STRAIGHT
TALK

STRAIGHT
TALK

Straightalk — about being a teen from a teen

"Yossi"
E-mail: straightalkft2t@hotmail.com

TARGUM/FELDHEIM

First published 2004
Copyright © 2004 by Targum Press
ISBN 1-56871-321-5

Published by:
TARGUM PRESS, INC.
22700 W. Eleven Mile Rd.
Southfield, MI 48034
E-mail: targum@netvision.net.il
Fax: 888-298-9992
www.targum.com

Distributed by:
FELDHEIM PUBLISHERS
202 Airport Executive Park
Nanuet, NY 10954

Printing plates: "Frank," Jerusalem
Printed in Israel

OHR SOMAYACH INSTITUTIONS

Rav Mendel Weinbach

"The foundation of saintliness and the root of perfection in the service of God," writes Rabbi Moshe Chaim Luzzatto at the beginning of his classic *Mesillas Yesharim*, "lies in a man's coming to see clearly and to recognize as a truth the nature of his duty in the world and the end towards which he should direct his vision and his aspiration in all of his labors all the days of his life."

More than four centuries after these immortal words of Mussar were written we hear them echoed by a modern Jewish youth reflecting on his teenage years.

Yossi is the voice of a confused and sometimes rebellious generation. Parents and educators have for years been trying to tell teenagers what is written in this very insightful book. But this time they will hear from one of their own, someone who has experienced their hardships and who understands them, unobstructed by the handicap of a generation gap.

Whether it is in regard to relationships with parents and society or in analyzing the causes of youthful rebellion, Yossi can be relied upon to supply a perspective which will be helpful to the young reader, and perhaps to the older one as well! The author makes no pretense of offering the expert counsel of a veteran parent or educator. He is merely speaking to the members of his generation as a caring friend who has endured most of what they have and who has survived to help others.

It is with great pride that I applaud this work of a beloved *talmid*, which will undoubtedly help others of his generation to also enjoy a happy ending to their personal story.

Mendel Weinbach

Rabbi Mendel Weinbach
Rosh Hayeshiva

כ"ק אדמו"ר מבוסטון שליט"א
הרב לוי יצחק הלוי הורוויץ
עיה"ק ירושלים ת"ו
Grand Rabbi Levi I. Horowitz
The Bostoner Rebbe

The Bostoner Rebbe

ב"ה

The teen years are years of struggle. Teenagers struggle to define themselves and find a way to fit into the world. Their parents, educators, and friends struggle to understand them and help them. But emotions run strong, for the teens themselves and for those who want to help. That makes understanding difficult. And without understanding, help is nearly impossible.

The author, whom I have known well all his life, has produced a book that can be a great aid to understanding. He knows what the teens are experiencing — their doubts, worries, great joys and great pains, hopes, fears, successes, and failures. He describes all this in realistic terms — terms that will be recognized by the teens themselves, and will enlighten their helpers.

But this is not all. Our writer possesses, and expresses, practical wisdom. He can evaluate the challenges and give solid guidance based on sensitive insight. He is able to adopt and represent the point of view of the teens in a way that few if any professionals can. For these reasons I believe that this book is a very important contribution to all those who are living with teens. *Yehi ratzon* that this book should succeed in helping teens to develop richer Torah lives.

The Bostoner Rebbe

contents

preface

I t's really weird trying to write a book about teens while being one. I got the idea one morning while sitting with a close friend (who has written a few books!). I said, "IT WOULD BE SO COOL IF I COULD WRITE A BOOK." He asked me what I would write about. I thought for a few moments and said, "I walk into bookstores all the time and I'm always attracted to books with titles like 'Getting Rid of Depression,' 'Being Happy,' 'Solving All Your Problems'…since I'm an unhappy depressed teen with lots of problems. So I buy the book, but close it after a few pages with a feeling of utter depression. The title was right but that was about it! I couldn't relate to anything the guy was talking about."

So I decided to write a book, not about my own problems and

how I dealt and am dealing with them, since what works for me won't necessarily work for you. Rather, I have written a book from one teen to another with the hope that we will be able to relate to similar feelings and problems, and that you'll see that you're not alone out there. Maybe we can even help each other out a little by sharing ideas and worries with each other (you can write to me at straightalkft2t@hotmail.com). I know you're probably thinking to yourself, "This guy can't possibly know what I'm going through. He can't help." Well my answer is, you're probably right, maybe I can't help, but I'm pretty sure that we have thought along the same lines at one time or another, so give me a chance. You just might be surprised!

intro

You have a disease, a fatal one. Go ahead, try to deny it, but you have contracted a fatal disease with no possible cure. In fact, this disease kills 100 percent of the people who get it. But don't worry, you're not alone — every single person has it and everyone dies from it. Have you guessed its name yet? Life. Yeah — life. Think about it for a minute. It's a pretty morbid picture. But it's true, isn't it? Okay, most diseases kill quickly and life takes time — but what's the real difference? Every day is just one step closer to death.

The thought should shake you up a bit and get your mind rolling. What is wrong with this perspective?

Let's take a step back. Have you ever known a person given a finite short time left to live? Like a month? How do they react? Well, let's pretend that that person is you. After the shock, denial, and despair are put into perspective, you would want to do it all. Eat the best food there is to eat, sleep in the fanciest hotels. Whatever you can physically do, enjoy, accomplish, hear… a mad dash to get it all in, in the few remaining days that you have left. Now, imagine, after all that, the doctor calls and tells you that he mixed up your chart with someone else's. You are fine, his deepest apologies. Can the feeling be described? Relief, gratitude, ecstasy. You think, "Wow, I can go back to regular life." Now isn't that ironic? When you had only thirty days left, you had not a moment to lose. Now that you have thirty years everything goes back to normal. But all of a sudden it hits that thirty years is just thirty days over and over again. It really is the same, unless… unless what? Why isn't life a slow-acting fatal disease?

Once more let us take a step back. When you thought you only had thirty days, why didn't you just say, "Kill me now"? What is the point if you only have thirty more days? Fine, you got to see Hawaii and the Eiffel Tower, ski the Alps and scuba dive in the Red Sea. But even if you get to see everything, you are going to die in thirty days. So what is the point? Well again, thirty days in thirty days or thirty days in thirty years — when it's over, it's over. So what's the point?

Why isn't life like any other fatal disease?

Well, do you see the point? Pardon the pun, but the point is that there is a point. Or, in other words, a goal. Goals? Yeah — goals. Let me explain. What would you call a bunch of men running around on a hot summer day up and down a blacktop lot for hours on end? Back and forth twenty, thirty times, running harder and harder, the sweat pouring down their faces. They seem like they are about to collapse from exhaustion. What would you call them? Subjects of pain, extreme torture. Look at them sweating, they must be in pain, how could anybody go on like that? But wait, they are smiling. How is this possible? Okay, it's not torture; no one is forcing them to do it. They must be insane or…just playing basketball. What happened? One orange sphere, a ball, and…? Ah, a net (or two), a hoop, a…goal, a point, a purpose.

Life isn't a disease, it's an opportunity. No goals — opportunity wasted. No point — it's just a slow process of decay. Find the goal, find the point, and you have got yourself a chance called a lifetime.

So now what? Now that we know this powerful information — now what? Are we going to live our life as thirty years or thirty days? How are we going to approach it?

Just like the game. A real game has a time limit, it has to end. (Even pickup games end at a certain point.) Without a time limit the definition of the goal loses its razor sharpness. That clock don't wait for nobody. Quick, help! Time is running — what do I do? Accept the challenge of asking yourself, and answering, these two questions. 1) What am I living for? 2) What am I doing about it? (I recently heard a story: During that terrible disaster on September 11, there was a cripple who was stuck on one of the higher floors of the building and couldn't get down. A person who saw him sitting there picked him up and carried him down dozens of flights of stairs leading him to safety. When they got out, the cripple looked up at the stranger and said, "You saved my life. How can I ever repay you?" The person replied, "Live your life the way a life is supposed to be lived. Make it a life worth saving.")

Knowing your purpose for being is the prerequisite for amazing living. Not just an amazing life, but amazing living. Not just mediocrity — but a constant fulfillment and continuous happiness. If you don't ask these questions, you can never get started.

I'd like to leave you with a question, because searching is part of the goal. When all is said and done, life does come to an end. We may have had good times — loved and been loved, worked for a purpose and accomplished, maybe even diverted the course of history, or left a mark in the world. Close your eyes and open your mind. What was the point? What meaning do my personal goals have if I am no more… is it really all over?

We live in a time when the pressures are strong and persuasive. Life itself, when looked at the wrong way, can be very depressing. A lot of people turn to religion in the hope of finding answers and direction for a meaningful life. Sometimes for those of us who are FFB the answers don't seem to be there. Our lives are filled with confusion. We look around at people who were not religious or Jewish and wonder:

1. Why do they want to take upon themselves this lifestyle with all the commitment and hardship?

2. How come they seem so happy?

Deep down we know that without religion our lives are meaningless. Yet, with it, all we seem to have is a life full of questions and no answers. There must have been a reason why we were put on this earth. Or maybe it was only by chance? That is really up to you to decide. When you look at your life until now do you wonder about if you accomplished anything? Did you waste your time? You know that you have a job to accomplish down here. Part of that job is to find out what your job is. When you look back at your life and ask "Was it worth it?" the answer has to be "Yes."

part one

why we rebel

why we rebel

Do you hate your parents? I'm sure it's happened to some of you, after a fight as you run to your room and slam the door shut, that you think to yourself, "I hate them." Do you mean it? Do you even have a right to say it?

There are many reasons why teenagers are not happy. As we get older, we are faced with problems and decisions that we never had to deal with before. We start to form our own opinions and ideas about how we want to live our lives. We also have to deal with our parents, siblings, school, society, friends, and most of all, ourselves.

Everyone's parents are different. Some care, while others don't. The parents who do care don't always know how to show it. The ones who don't care may be in need of care themselves.

I have come to my own conclusion that most parents really do care very much, but we think they don't. I mean, if they did care about us then they would let us do what we want! They wouldn't put restrictions on us! The problem is that they think that they know what is going on in the world but hey, they're from a different generation, and times have changed. They think that they always know what is best for us. I'm sure you've heard before, "It's just that I don't want you to make the same mistakes that I made." Well, for their information, sometimes we have to.

If they really cared, why do they have to make a big deal out of every little thing, like the way we dress, our hairstyle, what time we come home at night, or even who our friends are?

I think that the reason we have all these problems is because our parents really do care about us and love us. Therefore they also have expectations for us. You probably won't agree (right now) with the next thing I'm about to say, but you're lucky to have these problems. It means your parents do care about you, and parents who care can be worked with. If you don't have these problems it's because your parents don't care enough.

Your parents tried to instill certain qualities in you while you were growing up and they expect you to act accordingly. A lot of times what they expect isn't fair or doesn't seem fair, while there are other times when we should be doing things without even being told. So who's the problem, who's at fault? Us or our parents?

Have you ever wondered why it is that some kids are so messed up, especially kids from really good families, and other kids aren't? You would think that someone whose parent is a principal or a shrink would come out all right. If so, why is it that kids are straying so far from the way that their parents raised them?

I think the answer is that, ultimately, it's you who is going to decide the course of your life.

There are many reasons why we "rebel" against our parents. One reason is because they put too much pressure on us and expect too much. I remember one time I missed the bus to school in the morning. My mother got so upset at me that for the next month I had a 9 p.m. curfew! Now if you really want to know what happened, I had an electric alarm clock and the electricity blew during the night and it reset my alarm. Do you think that when I told my mother that, it changed anything from her point of view? Of course not. All she saw was that I missed the bus.

So, of course, I got upset at her and decided that there was no point in trying to be good and do the right thing if every time I tried, I got in trouble. I started missing school and cutting classes, and eventually what happened was that now I was not only in trouble with my parents but with school also. I got kicked out of school and things went from bad to worse, and all because of a stupid alarm clock. If I had only thought for a moment before reacting and said to myself, "Okay, she is making a big deal out of it, but I know it's because she really wants me to keep up in class," none of this would ever have happened.

Someone whose parents don't care about them will never have these problems because nothing is expected of them. If, by chance, he doesn't get up one morning, he will get up the next. Granted, having parents who don't care isn't a preferable alternative, for although they might not put restrictions on you, you're basically all alone. If this is the case then it's totally up to you to decide if you want to be good or not.

Another reason why a teen might "rebel" is because we are embarrassed by who our parents are and their positions in the community. We therefore try to prove to people that we are not like our parents. I mean, who would want to be your friend if you are the son or daughter of their teacher? If your parent has a high position you might be fed up, not with what your parents expect of you, but with what other people expect of you or think of you because of who your parents are. In other words, they have unrealistic expectations based on who your parents are, not who you are.

It's really funny how when we were little kids we used to always fight and argue about whose daddy is stronger. As kids we all looked up to our parents. Just to give a personal example: I remember looking through a filing cabinet in my house one time. I came across an essay that I wrote in second grade. Its title was "The Person I Admire Most." Of course I figured that I wrote about myself, but I was wrong. I had written about my mother. My mother! What was I thinking? So I guess, as we grow older, we don't really appreciate our parents as much as we did when we were growing up. Why is that? What causes us to forget or throw out the reasons we looked up to our parents?

Well, based on what we just said, because of 1) too much pressure, or 2) being embarrassed by who are parents are, or 3) not being looked at as an individual — these things can definitely cause us to move away from our parents and their lives. We didn't have these problems when we were growing up, because when you are little individuality isn't always such a big thing, and your parents' jobs don't really affect your life when you're six.

Feeling that you are an individual is very important, so when we feel that our parents don't recognize us as one, we try to go out of our way to feel like one, namely by doing things that our parents wouldn't approve of and not listening to them. (Sometimes our parents get so involved with their social standings that they don't spend enough time with us. I remember hearing about a very successful person whose son started taking drugs. Some people approached him and asked, "Isn't the apple not supposed to fall far from the tree?" He said back to them, "It depends how high the tree is." So you see, sometimes parents are so involved with helping others or with their own issues that they don't give their own kids the time that they need.)

Yet one has to wonder what really changed from when we were little kids to now? When did we start feeling that our parents don't care?

growing up

When you were a little kid, life was simple. You ate, slept, and made a mess in your diaper. As you got older you went to kindergarten, drew pictures, played, had a nap time, and overall felt pretty busy and content. Now, as a teen, you're like a baby again, except that now your room needs a change rather than your diaper! But there are more differences. Now you have to decide what to wear and eat instead of mommy doing it for you. It would make sense then for you to decide who your friends are and what time you should go to sleep. If so, why do our parents butt in?

Well, who is the one who drives you places and makes your doctor appointments? Who pays for your clothing and food? The answer is obvious. You wouldn't be able to do most of those things on your own. (It's so funny that all kids, no matter how old they are, ask their mother to call the doctor for them to make an appointment!) There will come a time when you will have to. So, it's safe to say that your parents feel that they are still able to make decisions about what time you should go to sleep. I'm pretty sure that if you get up on time every morning after going to bed at 12 that your parents will let you stay up till 12.

Sometimes they want you home because of safety. Now, to be honest with you, the times my parents said that they thought a friend of mine was a bad influence on me, they were right and I knew it. Of course I didn't let them know that! It pains them to see us doing something that they know will hurt us later. Let me ask you: if you took a test and the teacher asked a hard question, wouldn't you warn your friends? Sure you would, because you want them to succeed even if you didn't (if you're a true friend)! Now I'm not saying parents are always right. All of us have to make mistakes. We learn from our mistakes, just like our parents did. That's what makes us into better people. And we all know that no matter what our parents say, we are going to do what we want anyway. I once heard a lecturer say to parents " If you always say "No", why should your kid listen to you?" He was right!

Why is it that when you don't help at home you get yelled at? Yet, when you do help, no one ever says thank you? If your father comes in after a long day of work and your mom starts to complain about how messy the house is, you better hope the dishes are washed because otherwise you are going to be doing them. How many times have you seen your father wash the dishes or help at home? Don't ever try to bring that topic up, I guarantee you won't be able to sit for a week by the time he's finished with you! He'll give you the whole speech about how he is out all day trying to make a living and how your mother shouldn't have to clean up everyone else's mess. While he is saying this you're probably thinking to yourself, "I have five siblings. Why should I have to clean up after them? These aren't my dishes." (You don't say this, of course, since you already can't sit down because of the last beating.) It is always a big problem when our parents tell us to act one way, yet they act another. A father who never helps should not be telling you to help.

On the other hand, a mother who does all the work has a right to ask for a little help. You would be frustrated, too, if for the last fifteen years you changed diapers, didn't sleep, made meals and gave someone everything they needed, and, now, when they are old enough to give back, they don't. I think the problem is that when your mother is under so much stress all she sees is the mess, not what you did. If you tried a little not to let the house get so messy in the first place, your help would be noticed. I regret that it took me nineteen years to realize this. Now when I take out the garbage I can even smile sometimes. I realize that deep down my parents do care about me; all I had to do was look past the external stuff, like keeping my room clean. If so, why did I believe that they didn't care, for so long?

To reiterate, some parents don't practice what they preach. They tell you not to do something, yet they do it themselves, like staying up late watching TV or not cleaning up after they eat. So we think to ourselves, if they can do it, why can't we? Another very true and sad fact is that most of our parents have no clue about what is going on in our lives. Do you think that your parents know you well? This is another reason to feel that they don't care. Overall, parents can be very confusing. A friend of mine once told me about a conversation he had with his dad. It went something like this: "Dad, I know you don't like me going to the bar, but I'm going and I'll be back at 12." "Son, you know I don't approve of you going there!" "Dad, would you rather me lie to you and tell you I'm going somewhere else?"

"So you see," he said, "they always want you to be honest with them, and when you are, they get upset at you instead of thanking you for being honest with them."

Did you ever notice that parents make a big issue about everything, especially small things that are important to us like the way we dress? (We'll talk about that later.) There is still more. No kid likes to feel pressure even if it's for his own good. We, therefore, naturally do exactly the opposite of what our parents want us to do. The more pressure they put on us to succeed in school, the less we try. Some of us are happy with an 80 percent but parents don't seem to care about what we want. Not every kid wants to or is meant to be the best, but our parents forget about us.

By now most of you are probably saying to yourselves that I just described your parents. They are the ones who don't care. Whenever you go to a friend's house you always wonder why your parents can't be like his. The truth is, parents do care. Sometimes it's very easy to see it by other people's parents. They will never slap you or yell at you. Try to understand your parents and give them a chance. Put yourself in their shoes, you might see things a little differently.

So, after all this, when you storm up to your room and say, "I hate them," do you mean it? Think for a minute about why you're upset. Is it because they care about you and are pushing you too hard? Or is it because you don't feel appreciated? Calm down, take a deep breath, and ask yourself if you really hate your parents.

society

To all those blissfully unaware individuals, there is an entity called society. Though I'm not quite sure of its definition, I do know that people conduct themselves based on societal parameters in order to fit in. If you don't follow what society says, you won't fit in. For example, if you live in a place where everyone has a beard and you want to fit in, you have to grow a beard. If you decide that you want to shave you have separated yourself from that society. We all know that there is nothing wrong with not having a beard, but that's what that society decided.

Society decides what we should wear, which parties to go to, with whom to associate… I don't know who gave "them" or whoever they are this right to decide how we should live our lives. Nevertheless, the worst thing you can possibly think to yourself is "I'm going to change society," because you can't! It's impossible.

When your parents chose a place to live, they made their decision based on which society they wanted themselves and their kids to join. They raised you to fit into that society. Naturally, if all the people smoked pot your parents did too. If you live in a high-class community then you probably have a big house and at least three cars.

The way I see it, there are two reasons why not to like the place you live in. 1) You think that you are better than the people who live there and you look down on them. 2) You don't find that life appealing. To illustrate: if you live in Kansas on a farm, which your dad got from his dad…your life is pretty simple. Wake up at 4:30 a.m. to milk the cows, plow the fields, etc. Your mother grows vegetables. This is how your parents were brought up and they are satisfied with this way of life. They also probably brought you up this way. Now if you're an academically oriented person you might not feel fulfillment from this type of lifestyle. You might want to pursue a university degree and a professional career. This isn't because you disagree with the lifestyle and look down on your parents. It's just that you feel you can do more with your brains than raise sheep. Most parents would probably be happy if their child made a decision like that. It would earn their respect.

If you live in a rich stuck-up community where everyone wears the fanciest clothing and has shoes to match every outfit, you might feel that these people have no life aside from having so much money that they don't even know what to spend it on. (Personally I agree with you. I mean do you think that they are happy because they can buy a new car every day?) So you might want to pursue a more meaningful life where you feel that you are actually not wasting whatever time you have on this earth in garbage.

Your parents' attitude towards you is dependent on which society they've joined. If your parents have money, great jobs, and go to parties and luncheons all the time, they will probably assume that you're happy. After all, you have everything you could ever want. If their lives' goal is to make as much money as possible, they probably won't understand your inner feelings, even if you expressed your emotions to them. Yet, on the other hand, if your parents are poor and have to work extra hours just to make ends meet, you probably are expected to do a lot of things at home that most kids your age don't have to do. This can also lead to resentment.

It's a messed-up world where nobody is happy. People who don't have money want it. People who have it want more. They don't realize that they will never have enough to make them happy. It won't make a difference if you put the unhappy rich kid in the poor kid's place or vice versa. It's not where you are or what you have that will make you happy, but who you are! The problem is that people have a tendency to turn to money to solve their problems.

I'd like to share with you a story that blew my mind away. There was a man who had three sons. When his first son turned eighteen, the son received a letter from the family lawyer which contained a check for one million dollars. The family was overjoyed. The father asked the lawyer who sent it, but the lawyer said the man didn't want his name revealed. That son bought a fast car and ended up dying in a car crash. When the next son turned eighteen he also received a letter containing a check for one million dollars. He ended up getting involved with the wrong crowd, overdosed on drugs, and is currently a vegetable in some institution. When the third son turned eighteen and the same thing happened, the father told the lawyer that they didn't want the money. The lawyer said, "It's your son's money, he can take it if he wants." The father begged the lawyer to at least tell him who sent the money. The lawyer said: "Remember a few years ago, you had a bad breakup with your business partner? Well, he swore revenge and he felt that the best way to get back at you was to send each one of your sons on his eighteenth birthday one million dollars."

35

This hits real deep. I can't think of more to say about it.

So, as you can see, your parents' attitude towards you and their expectations vary depending on which society you live in, but your happiness is dependent only on you. I think that the biggest problem with parents is that they think that we are happy. After all, we don't go telling them that we're not. I've always wondered what would happen if kids were open with their parents. I'm pretty sure that most of the things that we have spoken about and will speak about wouldn't happen.

At first most of us try to fit into our surroundings, like we did when we were kids. As we mature we develop different emotions, partially due to hormonal changes. We live in a world which exerts a major pull to the physical world, namely TV, movies, music... even though many of us were brought up in a cloistered environment. Some kids will go through a stage when they feel the need to wear funky clothing or a crazy hairstyle. The problem is that when we go through this phase, our parents make a bigger deal out of it than it is, without understanding our motivations. It's normal for a kid to do funky things, and I'll bet that most of our parents did them, too. Instead of being understood, we get looked at like "bums" or "punks." This eventually makes us feel compelled to live up to the names that we are given because we live in a society where we aren't understood.

talking to parents

Why don't we talk to our parents?

Probably because we don't think that they will understand. But, even more so, because we don't think that they will approve! A friend of mine came over to me once and told me that the night before, he had been talking to his dad. His dad wanted to be his friend. He said to his father, "Friends can talk about everything. We can't." His father said back to him, "The only things that you feel you can't talk to me about are things that you know I think are wrong."

This is very true. I mean who would want to tell their parents things which they know would upset them? The problem is, if we can't talk to our parents about how we are feeling, then they can't understand why we feel the way we do.

There are two types of people: thinkers and non-thinkers. What I mean by this is that some kids will follow in the way of their parents without ever asking them "Why should I do this?" This can be good because when it comes to what's right and wrong, all you have to do is do what your parents tell you. On the other hand, you are just walking through life without learning how to live it! Someone who is a thinker will question his parents about why something is wrong, and why he should be doing what they ask.

This way has its advantages, because when you do find an answer, it will mean a lot more to you. For example, if one's parents say, "Don't take drugs," the one who just obeys says, "Okay, my parents know better." The thinker who wants to learn says, "Why not?" If the thinker goes and checks out why drugs are bad for you, he will then have a much greater understanding of why not to take drugs. On the other hand, the thinker will not always find people who can answer his question right away and, therefore, might end up doing things which he shouldn't be doing. The reason a lot of us have our problems is because we are thinkers and we don't find the right answers to our questions. Another problem is that we don't even ask our parents questions since we believe that they won't approve of the question (for example, asking "What's so bad about getting high and having fun?"). We don't ask them and instead we do whatever we want.

Let me tell you a story. Joe was a boy who lived in a very strict society (use your imagination!). The dress code was very simple, black pants and a white shirt. Schools were separate. Boys weren't allowed to hang out with girls at all. Listening to rap was a definite no-no. Well you see, our friend Joe was an average American fourteen-year-old who wanted to dress casually and have a girlfriend. He never spoke to his parents about it because he figured that they wouldn't understand him. So, he started sneaking out at night to hang out with some guys who felt the same way he did. As this went on, Joe was getting more and more depressed. You see, some people can go crazy if they feel that they are living a lie, having a double identity. You can never be happy with who you are, if you don't know who you are! Joe got very lucky. He managed to find someone who helped him figure out what was bothering him and gave him ideas about how to fix them. The next day, Joe came home in jeans and a T-shirt… His father didn't pull a gun on him as Joe expected he would. His mother, of course, started crying. They spoke for six hours! Joe realized that his parents had no clue as to what was going on in his life. They didn't see the problems he had; he never let them. They were hurt because they saw a boy who seemed to fit in and whom they thought was happy. Now they saw the real him: an angry, confused, unhappy teenager. It hurt them so much because they cared, and they just realized that they didn't even know their own son.

Joe is a made-up story. Yet how made-up is he really? Can you understand Joe? Why didn't he ever go to his parents and ask them to buy him a pair of jeans? Why did he have to go and mess up his life? Why do we hurt ourselves?

A lot of us think that if we have anger inside we can deal with it by letting it out. It's crazy, but people actually go and slice themselves on purpose, the idea being to try and focus all the pain on one spot. I remember when I was little, that whenever I was angry I would punch the walls. It didn't help. Anger isn't something that we can barbarically vent or tuck away. It has to be properly dealt with. One major way is by talking. If you are angry with a parent or friend, and instead of telling them that you are angry with them, you hit the wall ten times, you will still be angry with them and they won't have a clue why. You can hit your fist against the wall till your knuckles bleed, but every time you see that friend or parent you will be angry with them. The only way to solve this problem is by letting them know that you are mad at them, or by putting yourself in their place and seeing if you have a right to be angry with them or not. By talking, you are getting all your feelings off your chest.

Being honest is very hard, but it's the best way for a healthy relationship with someone, especially yourself. When we don't let our parents know what's eating us up inside, the pain just grows. Yet, it seems that we have a great reason for not wanting to talk to our parents. They won't approve and will only get upset.

Parents, teachers, and friends are human and can say things that they don't mean. Someone told me that in parenting classes they teach you never to say, "You're a bad girl" or " You're terrible." Kids take offense very easily at what people say, and we shouldn't. I remember a story my friend told me about how he went to hear a lecture when he was in South Africa. At the end of the lecture he asked the lecturer a few questions. The lecturer said, "I see from your questions that you will never amount to anything." After hearing that from a well-known lecturer he became very depressed. He started drinking and stopped going to school. A few years later this boy bumped into that same lecturer, and said, "Hi, do you remember me? I heard you speak in South Africa." The lecturer said, "Sorry, but I have no clue who you are." So, you see sometimes, people say things without meaning or knowing what they are saying. If we take everything that people say personally, we can really get hurt. The effect of criticizing words really depends on the speaker. When a close caring friend tells you that you've done something bad, they don't mean that you are bad. They are giving you criticism, which you are supposed to learn from, because they care about you. If a person who doesn't know you says that you are terrible, worthless, or stupid, just ignore it. They don't know you and can't come to such a conclusion. A person who doesn't know you can tell you that what you did was bad, but not that you are bad.

We all know that a lot of times parents yell or get upset at us for no apparent reason. They can sometimes say things which are very hurtful. The reaction of any normal person is to stay away from someone who hurts you. Has it ever happened that you told your parents about something bad that you did, like fail a test? At the time they were cool with it and really didn't react. A month later you do something which upsets them, and all of a sudden they are yelling at you about how poorly you do at school…

If whenever we tell them something they use it against us, what is the point of telling them anything at all?

problems with having parents

1. Parents make big mistakes.

et me tell you what happened to a girl I knew in our neighborhood. When she turned sixteen she started wearing what people might call "revealing" clothes. Her parents, who favored a more modest wardrobe, were shocked at her behavior. They called her lots of not nice names and said that she was an embarrassment to their family. Over the next few months a change could be seen in this girl. The once always-smiling, happy-go-lucky girl was now looking like garbage. She started hanging out with the wrong people and getting into a mess.

About two years after she started "bugging out" I got a call from her. All I heard on the phone for five minutes was crying, but I knew it was her. When she was finally able to speak she told me that she was in the hospital due to an overdose of alcohol and sleeping pills. She didn't have any contact with family or friends and asked if I would mind coming over. When I got to her room I didn't recognize her. I could hardly look at her.

She looked sickening. I made myself look at her and with a forced smile said, "Hi." For the next hour and a half she cried about all the mistakes she had made and how she wished she could just take it all back. She hated all the people who she thought were her friends and missed her family whom she hadn't seen in over a year. So I asked her a simple question, "Why not start over again?" Her answer was shocking. She said, "I can't change who I am." (It's shocking because this was one of the best people I knew who happened to go through a tough time. She really believed that she was bad; she had internalized this feeling of worthlessness.)

This story has a happy ending, unlike so many others. When she got out of the hospital she went to rehab for five months. During that time a friend of mine who is in charge of an institution for kids with cancer asked me if I knew any people who would spend time with these kids. I called my friend in rehab and she said that she would give it a shot. About two months later she invited me to her nineteenth birthday party. When I arrived I was shocked. Her parents were there! She was smiling! All the little kids who had cancer were there holding on to her. Later on, she told me that working with these kids gave her a motive to live again. She realized how precious life was and that she was lucky to be healthy. She also realized that there was a lot of good in her to give to others.

She also told me something that I'll never forget. She said, "If my parents hadn't made such a big deal about my clothes, I probably would have stopped wearing them. I didn't even like the way I looked in them. It's just that my friends pushed me to try something new. After my parents called me all those names, I felt that that's who I was and I couldn't change it. I was never happy during the two years I was away from home. I knew I wasn't a bad person but I acted like one anyway. If only I could have spoken to my parents about it, everything might have turned out differently."

Now, if you ask me, I think her parents were wrong with the way they reacted about her clothing. They put their own feelings before their daughter's. As understandable as it is that parents can be upset by the impression their children make on others, they must also take into account how we feel about it. We also have to realize that it's very important to our parents what others think about us. This is because our parents care about what others will say regarding their children. A lot of times we blow things out of proportion and cause ourselves a lot of unnecessary pain. If both our parents and we could learn when to give in, everything would be much smoother and many disputes would never occur.

2. They never give in.

The problem is that we think our parents should give in and they think that we should. It always seems that it's we who are giving in and not them. Even if they gave in sometimes, there would be a major improvement in our relationship with our parents.

I remember when I was seventeen my parents always made a fuss if I left the house with my shirt untucked. They felt that I looked messy. I felt comfortable that way. Every time I left the house we would fight about it. Finally I decided that when I left the house I would tuck it in and when I got outside I would untuck it. This way I avoided a stupid fight. This doesn't mean that I agreed with my parents or that they were right. But if I give in on small things, I thought, maybe they will hear me out on the bigger ones.

But the idea behind giving in doesn't mean that we should let our parents think we are doing one thing while we really are doing something else. Rather it means to try and listen to what your parents are saying. I was wrong because I didn't get a better understanding of why my parents felt a shirt should be tucked in. The argument was still there, I just tried avoiding it. Giving in just to avoid a fight isn't the right reason for giving in. You have to try to understand what they are saying and be considerate even if you know that they aren't right or making any sense.

3. They are never wrong.

want to ask you a question, be honest! What are the percentage of times that your parents are right about whatever it may be? To answer my own question I would have to say that my parents are right 95 to 99 percent of the time. If so then according to logic I should listen to them. I think that from when I was fourteen to eighteen I listened to them one out of every thirty times. I think

47

that the main reason that we don't listen to them is because they are always right. Nobody likes the kid in school who has all the answers and gets 100 on every test. To be honest, my brother is always right. Therefore, I never argue with him because I hate losing. Many times we go against what we know is right just to try and prove our parents wrong.

Another reason we don't listen to our parents is because when they are wrong, they can't admit it. It makes them feel weak if they have to tell their kid that they were wrong. Naturally, when we are wrong we won't admit it either.

Most of all, I believe that we need to feel like individuals. If we let our parents tell us what to do and make our decisions for us then we don't feel that we are in charge of what happens in our life. So of course we do our own thing. Most of the time we don't even enjoy what we are doing.

Did you ever feel that little pang of guilt after you did something that your parents wouldn't approve of? That would be your conscience. It is telling you that you are really better than the way you have been behaving. You might think that you are not, but I don't know anyone who woke up one morning and decided to pierce every part of his body and take drugs just for kicks. It's a gradual process that started somewhere. So in the beginning when we do things that we know we shouldn't be doing, we feel bad. If you do these things long enough, you will lose who you really are and not only feel like nothing, but become a nothing. You won't solve your problems by believing you are somebody that you really aren't. We all have good inside of us; we can't let other people make us lose ourselves.

So, right now, ask yourself, "Are you happy?" Do you feel that you are a better person than you appear to be? I think the answer to this last question is yes. You know that you can improve your life. It definitely isn't easy, but it's possible. So now you have a choice to make: either live your life as it has been up till now and always think what could have been. Or do something about it. What do you really want?

In order to answer this last question you have to put everything else aside. The same way you decided to forget about your parents and society, you have to set aside your friends and reputation. If you want to be happy you have to think about what you want and not what your friends will think. If you think that by doing the right thing you will lose friends, I hate to break it to you, but those aren't true friends. A real friend will probably be jealous of the move you made and might snap out of what he is doing because of you. It's really lousy to feel depressed and confused all the time. There seems to be no reason to continue living, when it feels like life can't get better.

But it can! It won't be easy but it's possible. The first step is to decide what you want out of life. If you've given up, then it's all over. Once you decide that you want to improve the way things have been going, and you realize that there is what to work on and change, then you are definitely on your way. What the heck are you waiting for? Do something about it!

part two

finding yourself

finding yourself

Who are you?

Has it ever happened that you woke up one morning and looked into the mirror, and asked yourself, "Who am I?" Do you even recognize the face staring back at you? Sometimes we are disgusted by what we see. It's funny, yet almost everyone I asked who claimed to be unhappy admitted that at one time or another they stood in front of a mirror and made faces at it to see what they would look like if they ever smiled. Have you ever sat down with a bunch of pictures from your childhood and wondered how that person in the picture could be you; I mean you look so happy.

We all think a lot and have different emotions and feelings coursing through our minds all the time. This can be very frustrating and confusing since most of the time we can't even point a finger at exactly what is bothering us or why we feel specifically the way that we do. Yet one has to wonder: there was a beginning to this confusion. When did it start? Why did it start? These are questions you have to start asking yourself if you want to be able to look into that mirror, smile, and say, "That's me."

Have you ever wondered why sometimes you do the stupidest things just to impress somebody? I've seen guys walk around in the most bizarre circus-clown clothes just to get attention. (I mean, even a color-blind person would be able to see those colors!) I'm not talking, though, just about impressing people. I'm talking about trying to be accepted by others. Being accepted is a great feeling; being accepted by doing things that we don't believe in stinks. If you are "hanging out" with a group of people who won't accept you for who you are, then you shouldn't be hanging out with them. Although it is common for people to try to impress others by trying to be like them, this isn't always the case. Sometimes we try to impress people for no reason at all, people we don't even know! We lie a little about something or exaggerate a story for no obvious reason. Have you ever insinuated that you did something really bad when you didn't? Why? It's not embarrassing to be a good kid and behave properly. So why do we try to project a negative image instead of our true selves? Why are we embarrassed by our goodness?

Why we try to impress others

The thought of rejection is very painful. Be it in school or a relationship, no one ever wants to be turned down. The urge to be accepted is so great that we convince ourselves that a person will only accept us if we act like this. Well, one of two things will happen. They won't like you, or they will realize you're faking and won't like you either. The problem is that we have all seen so many movies where the good guy pretends to be a bad guy so that way he can fit in and uncover the plot. We start thinking, "Hey I can fake it." Think about it. The reason the good guy has to fake it is so that he can be with the bad guys. (Sure you have people who pretend to be good when they're not, like when trying to get into a good school, but that is usually for a good cause and to live up to what you are saying will make you a better person.) You have to fake it to be with bad people (most of them are faking it too).

Most of the time we are wrong when we try to anticipate what another person will think about us. There were so many times I tried to do things which I thought would impress people and it actually backfired. Yes, there are exceptions, but overall the way you walk or talk or dress won't make the difference. Just be yourself!

Why aren't so many people just being themselves? The most reasonable answer is because they don't like themselves. This is a massive problem that lots of people have. It's a scary fact. If we were comfortable with who we are, then life would be much more enjoyable because we would be doing things for ourselves. But because we aren't sure about who we are then nothing we do will make us happy because we'll never know if that's what we really want. Usually what ends up happening is that instead of trying to figure out who we are and what we want, we decide what others would want us to be.

If so, it's fair to say that the reason we care so much about what others will think of us is because we don't know who we really are, or we have low self-esteem. If we appreciated who we really are then what others think wouldn't be such a big deal.

Well you might be wondering, "How do you figure out who you are?" This is something I will hopefully write about later, but as not to keep you in suspense (since you've been such a patient reader to have gotten this far) the first step is to be honest with yourself. When you do something, ask yourself, "Why am I doing this? Am I doing this because I want to or because I'm worried about what the other person will think?" I'll let you in on a big secret: I've come to believe that if you can do something without thinking about it, then you are doing it for yourself. If you have to debate with yourself about what to do, then it's for others.

To clarify, just think about how much time some people spend in front of the mirror getting ready to go out — choosing just the right clothes or hairstyle so that they will make the best impression. The reason we have a hard time making a decision what to wear is because we care too much about what other people think. If you don't have to sit in front of a mirror for twenty minutes every time before you go out of the house, it's because you're not worried about what people will think of your appearance. (To be reasonable, if you are applying for a job, don't go in your pajamas. You have to look presentable, but be yourself. There is proper etiquette for every situation. There is a minimum standard of presentability a person must have.)

Who is "cool"?

When looking around at the people in school it seems that all the popular kids are the "cool" ones. When I say "cool," I mean the ones who smoke and dress real well. The ones who make trouble in class and are always getting into fights.

These are qualities that a lot of people don't possess. So if you want to be popular you probably think to yourself, "I have to be cool." Well how do you become cool? It's really easy, take every good quality you have and trash it. Start to curse and smoke, maybe buy some new clothing and jewelry and "voila" you're cool.

As you make your new friends you will probably start to realize that they aren't as great as you thought. They're more like an inconsiderate, irresponsible gang of losers. (When I say losers I mean losing out on life. After all, "I" was one.) Most of this group is made up of kids with learning difficulties or problems at home. (This can include divorced parents or a kid who doesn't like the way his parents raised him religiously.) They use this image as an escape where they can feel good about themselves.

I learned a big lesson from my "cool" days. I realized that the reason one shows off is because he is insecure about himself and therefore has to publicize himself. People who don't get enough attention seek it through negative things, which in our stupidity we view as cool. The way I see it is, if you are really good at something people will notice without you telling them. Showing off is also really annoying to those around you. I remember one of my friends started cursing all the time. Every other word was a curse. After a while we all just stopped talking to him. I told him to be my friend he doesn't have to curse. "It doesn't even impress me," I said.

Being loud doesn't necessarily mean that you are in control. A principal in a school might seem to be in charge but he's not. There is a committee that decides how he has to run the school and what to spend money on. He is more like a puppet. It's also like that in a relationship. The man seems to be in charge, but really the woman always runs the show. A leader has to perform, but not always in a loud and noticeable way. As the saying goes, "Silence is golden."

To take it a step further. For every "why" there is a "what." What I mean by this is the following: We said before that a person might want to be cool. Why? Because he doesn't feel as if he has friends or because he feels that he is a bad kid (this is his reason). What really causes him to feel this way? Lack of self-esteem. Are you lacking in self-esteem? Well let me ask you, if I were to tell you, "Nice shirt," what would your response be? Would it be "Thank you" or "What, you don't like my shirt?" Of course the person with no self-esteem answers the latter. So if you want to find the real reason and root of why kids go and do bad stuff, you have to find the "what."

Most of the time it can be traced back to a lack of self-value. This can definitely be caused by a learning disability, which causes a kid to think that he is stupid. Or by having problems at home and not feeling loved. These are legitimate reasons for feeling bad about yourself, but drugs aren't the answer and won't make you feel better about yourself. If you don't fall into the two categories I've mentioned (learning disability or problems at home) then your problem, most likely, is in the way you perceive yourself and your outlook on life. (In the beginning drugs do seem to help and make you feel better. To say that they aren't enjoyable would be a lie. A lot of us just want to experience the pleasures of things, which are unknown to us. If we understand why people turn to drugs and the effect which they have on us, maybe we would look for other options first.)

So you want to know who is cool? It's the person who has friends who like him for who he is. It's the girl who can feel good about herself and smile. It's the person who doesn't have to smoke that cigarette to fit in. (Cool isn't only dependant on friends. A loner in a corrupt society of losers is also "cool.") In order to be one of these people you have to like yourself. But first, you must get to know yourself. Let's take a look at a few areas where people tend to put themselves down and without even knowing it, majorly impact their lives and way of thinking.

measuring ourselves against others

Ever look around at everyone else and feel jealous? Whether in school, after you studied so hard and only got an 80 percent, while some other kid didn't even study and did much better than you. Or when some kids wear the newest coolest designer clothes, while you have been wearing the same old pair of pants for the last two years?

If so, I'm sorry to inform you that you're normal. I mean it's not fair that your friends have their own cars, laptops, and anything they want while you still have to ride your bike to school. The fact that their parents have money and yours don't is out of your hands.

In eleventh grade I was considered a pretty popular guy. I was never able to understand why these rich kids wanted to be my friends. Okay, I wasn't stupid, I'm pretty good looking, I made the clothes I had look good, but they had everything! I realized that money can't buy you friends or a personality. It's not the clothes you wear or what you smoke that makes you happy or popular, maybe only at first glance. If you're lucky, you should be jealous of the people who are happy, not the ones who have money or seem to be cool. All the kids who I thought were "losers" when I was younger are some of the nicest and best people I know.

When we start looking at what others have, we not only forget what we have — we start to believe that we don't have anything at all. Everyone has good qualities in them but you lose them when you try to be someone you're not. This might sound really far off, but someone once told me, "You're not what you think you are. You're not what others think you are. You are what you think others think you are." This means that just because you think you're nice doesn't mean that you are. If others think you are an idiot, that doesn't make you one. If you think that your friends think that you are a great person, then you really are.

When we compare the progress of others to our own lack of achievement, it's tempting to feel that we're not successful at all. After all, you both put the same amount of time into what you're doing, yet he seems to be doing so much better. The simple solution seems to be to start working harder but, as you know, that doesn't really work. So we end up feeling very depressed since we don't feel accomplished at all. Imagine having a feeling of lack-of-achievement for a week, a month, or a year. Well we really don't have to imagine much since this is the way so many of us feel.

What does it mean if we are in an environment or system (school) where we don't feel that we are living up to the expectations of the place we are in? Usually we decide that it's a problem with the place we are in . "It wasn't the right place for me." Well let me let you in on a little secret. I went to four different schools in three years and in each place I had the same feeling of unachievement. So I decided to heck with school. I wasn't happy, I didn't feel as if I fit in to society. I didn't feel like a person. Not once did it ever occur to me that my goals for myself were way too high. Are your goals too high? Be honest, think about it for a minute, and then ask yourself why you never realized that your goals were too high? You probably won't be surprised if I tell you that you still think your goals are reachable. After all, you know better than anyone else what you are capable of doing. The big question is: "WHY AREN'T YOU DOING IT?"

goals

Using your potential

Has it ever happened that someone gave you a compliment and it bothered you? Like when your teacher told you that you had so much potential to be an outstanding student, or when you worked in a camp and one of your camper's parents told you how amazing and talented you were with kids. Yet, you thought to yourself, "I'm a bad person. I do so many things wrong; there is nothing good within me. These people must be nuts!"

Why do we belittle our actions and ourselves? Do we really believe that there is no good in us?

I believe that there is a lot of good in people who don't think they are good. I also believe that everyone knows his abilities. You might be a kind person, a great liar…it can all be used for positive things. A problem arises when we don't use our gifts to their full potential. For example: two different people give a dollar to charity. The poor person who gives a buck to charity used his kindness to its full potential. The rich person, who inside really is kind, will feel bad that he only gave one dollar to charity since he knows he can do so much more. Now, when the person collecting offers gratitude, saying, "Thank you for being so kind," the poor person feels that he was very kind since he gave as much as he could, but the rich guy doesn't feel kind at all. So you see two people can perform the same exact act, yet when thanked and complimented, one feels great and the other feels lousy. The reason is pretty clear. When the collector said, "You're so kind," he was telling the rich man what he already knew, that he is a kind person, but since he doesn't feel that he is being as kind as he should have been, it hurts. After a while he starts to believe that he isn't a nice person. The rich guy doesn't give money anymore; this is a comfort to him. Now he believes that he really is a bad person.

People set their goals based on what they think they are capable of doing. This is why we never think that our goals are too high, because we know what we can do. The problem is that if we aren't using our capabilities to their full potential we will never reach the goals that we set for ourselves. Setting goals is good and will make a person feel good about him or herself. Setting goals that we can't reach can destroy us. Only if we can feel good about who we are, will we ever be able to achieve. By setting goals which we can't reach, we end up depressed and stop setting goals for ourselves. This is why so many teenagers don't have any goals.

Thinking ahead

I f you wake up in the morning and your first thought is "Darn, not another day," then something is very wrong. If your daily schedule doesn't contain something new and exciting every day, life will be boring. By setting goals for yourself you will have something to strive for. It will also give you a feeling of achievement. But your goals must be realistic, so before you set a goal, think if your goal is too high.

It is indisputable that many people are depressed. I believe that a large part of the depression which many people experience is due to not having any goals. I'd like to share with you what my friend M. Back told me.

Depression is a common problem amongst teenagers. Regardless of social standing and financial situation, most teens do experience some degree of depression. Obviously someone who is a social outcast will show his depression more than someone who is popular and is depressed for different reasons. However, I believe that most depression can be traced to boredom or disenchantment with life. As a normal well-adjusted teenager, with plenty of friends and not lacking in anything monetary, I know that this theory holds true for me. Teens end up in a vicious cycle. They are chasing after things that they have been pressured into chasing by their friends, all in the pursuit of happiness. At the same time comes the disenchantment, to some extent, with the very things which they pursue. Hence the people who we look at as "geeks" are really the happiest, since they are pursuing what they really want.

The concept of doing something for a greater good, or even for purely selfish ambition, is not something which teenagers think about. As a child of the "popular" group, I remember trying to figure out why I was feeling depressed when nothing seemed to be wrong. Now, in my twenties, I have come to the conclusion that my depression was due to the mindset of that time. As a teenager, one has no material worries. Parents supply all your needs and life is based on instant gratification. Long-term goals are a concept which teens don't have to worry about. Therefore, the depression that a teen experiences is a depression of not getting instant gratification at that moment.

I think the reason teens are more depressed than other age groups is first of all because the teen years are most unstable. It is also much harder to follow a pattern of constantly having fun and partying, and then starting college or a job. Teenagers who reach the realization that it is realistically impossible to party all the time, will be better adjusted and will be much happier people.

happiness

Make others feel good

 used to think that if I made someone else happy, the feeling of happiness that I experienced wasn't my own. The only reason that I was feeling good was because I had made my friend feel good.

This isn't true. Since you're striving to bring happiness to others, you have to become one who radiates happiness. If you're sad there is no way that you're going to make someone else happy. It just won't work.

Someone who by nature is a jealous person will be negatively affected every time a person he knows has something good happen to him. Even though the fact that his friend got a new car isn't connected to him at all, he will be jealous.

Conversely, one who seeks to make others happy, who is constantly striving to bring happiness to others, the first one to benefit will be himself. By helping others, you are in fact really helping yourself.

It's very hard to feel that people value you. Usually all we feel is the negativity of others towards us. We always seem to dwell on the nasty things which people say and do to us, instead of focusing on the positive. We all have to know that people really do appreciate us, sometimes for things that we don't even know that we did.

I just read a story in a weekly newsletter which illustrates this point beautifully:

> One day, when I was a freshman in high school, I saw a kid from my class walking home from school. His name was Kyle. It looked like he was carrying all of his books. I thought to myself, "Why would anyone bring home all his books on a Friday? He must really be a nerd."
>
> I had quite a weekend planned (parties and a football game with my friends the next afternoon), so I shrugged my shoulders and went on. As I was walking, I saw a bunch of kids

running towards him. They ran at him, knocking all his books out of his arms and tripping him so he landed in the dirt. His glasses went flying, and I saw them land in the grass about ten feet from him. He looked up and I saw this terrible sadness in his eyes.

My heart went out to him. So, I jogged over to him, and, as he crawled around looking for his glasses, I saw a tear in his eye. As I handed him his glasses, I said, "Those guys are jerks. They really should get lives."

He looked up at me and said, "Hey thanks!" There was a big smile on his face. It was one of those smiles that showed real gratitude. I helped him pick up his books and asked him where he lived. As it turned out, he lived near me. I asked him why I had never seen him before. He told me that he had gone to a private school until now.

I would never have hung out with a private school kid before. We walked all the way home, and I carried some of his books. He turned out to be a pretty cool kid. I asked him if he wanted to play a little football with my friends. He said yes. We hung out the whole weekend, and the more I got to know Kyle, the more I liked him, and so did all my friends.

Monday morning came, and there was Kyle with the

huge stack of books again. I stopped him and said, "Boy, you are really gonna build some serious muscles with this pile of books every day!" He just laughed and handed me half the books.

Over the next four years, Kyle and I became best friends. When we were seniors, we began to think about college. Kyle decided on Georgetown, and I was going to Duke. I knew that we would always be friends, that the miles would never be a problem. He was going to be a doctor, and I was going for business on a football scholarship.

Kyle was valedictorian of our class. I teased him all the time about being a nerd. He had to prepare a speech for graduation. I was so glad it wasn't me having to get up there and speak.

Graduation day, I saw Kyle. He looked great. He was one of those guys that really found himself during high school. He filled out and actually looked good in glasses. He had more dates than I had, and, boy, sometimes I was jealous. Today was one of those days. I could see that he was nervous about his speech. So, I smacked him on the back and said, "Hey, big guy, you'll be great!" He looked at me with one of those looks (the really grateful one) and smiled. "Thanks," he said. As he started his speech, he cleared his throat, and began.

"Graduation is a time to thank those who helped you make it through those tough years. Your parents, your teachers, your siblings, maybe a coach…but mostly your friends. I am here to tell all of you that being a friend to someone is the best gift you can give them. I am going to tell you a story…"

I just looked at my friend with disbelief as he told the story of the first day we met. He had planned to kill himself over the weekend. He talked of how he had cleaned out his locker so his mom wouldn't have to do it later, and was carrying all his stuff home. He looked hard at me and gave me a little smile. "Thankfully, I was saved. My friend saved me from doing the unspeakable."

I heard the gasp go through the crowd as this handsome, popular boy told us all about his weakest moment. I saw his mom and dad looking at me and smiling that same grateful smile. Not until that moment did I realize its depth. Never underestimate the power of your actions. With one small gesture you can change a person's life, for better or for worse.

A lot of people are scared to say "thanks" because it means that you did something for them, and that makes them vulnerable.

If you start to appreciate yourself, you will be able to see that others really do appreciate you. All you have to know is how to tune into it.

All the good things

Reprinted from the Reader's Digest, with permission
Condensed from Proteus

Helen P. Mrosia

He was in my third-grade class. I taught at St. Mary's School in Morris, Minn. All thirty-four of my students were dear to me, but Mark Eklund was one in a million. Very neat in appearance, he had that happy-to-be-alive attitude that made even his occasional mischievousness delightful.

At the end of the year I was asked to teach junior-high math. The years flew by, and before I knew it, Mark was in my classroom again. He was more handsome than ever and just as polite. Since he had to listen carefully to my instructions in the "New Math," he did not talk as much in ninth grade as he had in third.

One Friday, things just didn't feel right. We had worked hard on a new concept all week, and I sensed that the students were growing frustrated with themselves and edgy with one another. I had to stop this crankiness before it got out of hand. So I asked them to list the names of the other students in the room on two sheets of paper, leaving a space between each name. Then I told them to think of the nicest thing they could say about each of their classmates and write it down.

It took the remainder of the class period to finish the assignment, but as the students left the room, each one handed me the papers. Charlie smiled. Mark said, "Thank you for teaching me, sister. Have a good weekend."

That Saturday, I wrote down the name of each student on a separate sheet of paper, and I listed what everyone else had said about that individual. On Monday I gave each student his or her list. Some of them ran two pages. Before long, the entire class was smiling. "Really?" I heard whispered. "I never knew that meant anything to anyone!"

"I didn't know others liked me so much!"

No one ever mentioned those papers in class again. I never knew if they discussed them after class or with their parents, but it didn't matter. The exercise had accomplished its purpose. The students were happy with themselves and one another again.

That group of students moved on. Several years later, after I returned from a vacation, my parents met me at the airport. As we were driving home, Mother asked the usual questions about the trip — the weather, my experiences in general. There was a slight lull in the conversation. Mother gave Dad a sideways glance and simply said, "Dad?" My father cleared his throat as he usually did before saying something important. "The Eklunds called last night," he began.

"Really?" I said. "I haven't heard from Mark in years. I wonder how Mark is."

Dad responded quietly. "Mark was killed in Vietnam," he said. "The funeral is tomorrow, and his parents would like it if you could attend." To this day I can still point to the exact spot on I-494 where Dad told me about Mark.

The church was packed with Mark's friends. Chuck's sister sang "The Battle Hymn of the Republic." Why did it have to rain on the day of the funeral? It was difficult enough at the graveside. The pastor said the usual prayers, and the bugler played taps.

I was the last one to bless the coffin. As I stood there, one of the soldiers who had acted as a pallbearer came up to me. "Were you Mark's math teacher?" he asked. I nodded as I continued to stare at the coffin. "Mark talked about you a lot," he said.

After the funeral, most of Mark's former classmates headed to Chuck's farmhouse for lunch. Mark's mother and father were there, obviously waiting for me. "We wanted to show you something," his father said, taking a wallet out of his pocket. "They found this on Mark when he was killed. We thought you might recognize it."

Opening the billfold, he carefully removed two worn pieces of notebook paper that had obviously been taped, folded, and refolded many times. I knew without looking that the papers were the ones on which I had listed all the good things each of Mark's classmates had said about him. "Thank you so much for doing that," Mark's mother said. "As you can see, Mark treasured it."

Mark's classmates started to gather around us. Charlie smiled rather sheepishly and said, "I still have my list. It's in the top drawer of my desk at home."

Chuck's wife said, "Chuck asked me to put his in our wedding album."

" I have mine, too," Marylyn said. "It's in my diary."

Then Vicki, another classmate, reached into her pocketbook, took out her wallet, and showed her worn and frazzled list to the group. "I carry this with me at all times," Vicki said without batting an eyelash. "I think we all saved our lists."

That's when I finally sat down and cried. I cried for Mark and for all his friends who would never see him again.

It really hits deep, it leaves a real and lasting impression, when one receives a well-deserved compliment. People appreciate being appreciated. If so we have to start appreciating ourselves. One way to do this is by minimizing our problems. This doesn't mean that our problems aren't real or serious, but let's put them into perspective. It would be unrealistic to make believe that everything is great and that's it (we'll look at that aspect of life later on). But am I not right that there is some good to focus on? If so think about it, write it down. Start to appreciate yourself a little.

Change your perspective

I heard this story from my friend, R.H.M.

All my problems were put into perspective by a hitchhiker I happened to pick up. (I love picking up hitchhikers. How can I pass by with an empty seat and let that sweet guy's soul whither out there?) We started talking, and I asked him where he's from… Turns out he's from the Soviet Union. He was a journalist. Accused of writing some anti-communist articles, he was sentenced to six years in prison.

"Wow," I said. "Really? Tell me what it's like in a Soviet prison." (I'm insatiably curious.)

His description was enough to make otherwise modest accommodations seem like a palace, almost like a dream. I don't remember all the details. I do recall, however, that it was anything but pleasant.

He even described with vivid detail what solitary confinement is like. You're in a tiny cell, the only place available to sit down is barely larger than a small tile, and you get to stare at the wall all day and contemplate your regrets at offending the ruling party, which has brought paradise upon the whole nation.

"How are you so familiar with solitary confinement?" I asked.

He explained that he was actually there. His seven-year-old daughter had written him a letter, and the prison manager would not let him see it, "For security reasons…"

He couldn't accept their reasoning — what security would be threatened by his daughter's letter? — and started getting wild.

No problem for them. Thirty-five days confinement.

The food wasn't great before, but now his meager rations were down to 800 calories a day. So, he decided, better not to eat at all. That way, after two or three days you forget about food, as opposed to eating a tiny bit, in which case your stomach will constantly nag you.

Well, a problem came up from an unexpected angle. Although it sounds funny, there was a law in the Soviet Union that you have to eat at least once every three days. So, if our hapless prisoner was planning to fast, he was actually transgressing the law.

They tried to force-feed him.

He clenched his teeth, not letting them put in food. Again, no problem. Evidently, they had some experience with such vicious, iniquitous lawbreakers. They handcuffed him and inserted between his clenched teeth a gadget which jerks the mouth open, forcefully. So forcefully, in fact, that all his teeth were knocked out.

I interrupted the story. "What do you mean, all your teeth were knocked out?"

The answer was short and needed no elaboration. It was to be understood, he said, quite literally. All the teeth now in his mouth were artificial. He promptly demonstrated by pulling out of his mouth a solid plate flanked by metallic teeth.

Continuing the process, they stuck a pipe down his now

wide-open mouth and were able to easily put food in, which slid straight down his esophagus. He would no longer fast more than three days. Hence, he would be properly abiding by the law.

This whole story also helps me put things in perspective. Do I have problems? Nah! The very worst thing I have is inconveniences. I once heard someone make a statement about such an approach: "If you're looking up, you're down. If you're looking down, you're up." It all depends on your perspective. If you're looking at people who are in a better situation than you are, then the contrast shows you as being in the negative, puts you down. If, however, you compare yourself to someone in a worse situation than yourself, then you aren't so bad off. It could have been a lot worse. IF YOU LOOK UP, YOU'RE DOWN. IF YOU LOOK DOWN, YOU'RE UP.

What is happiness?

 believe that every person wants to be happy. Most people wonder why they aren't happy. Usually we find reasons to explain our unhappiness or to justify it. We then try to find ways to make us happy. People turn to alcohol to forget their problems.

This doesn't make them happy, and when they sober up they are left with their unhappiness plus a nasty hangover. Drugs make you feel happy, they also put you in a different reality. This is only running away from yourself. If you can stay on drugs for the rest of your life you might be happy, you might not. Unmarried people turn to relationships because it makes them feel as if they have value; after all, someone finds you attractive. But having a relationship just to feel good about yourself is counterproductive. Using things or people to make us happy won't work, all it will do is get us more depressed. What's the answer? Commit suicide; it's the easiest way out of all your problems. Or maybe try to find out what happiness is. See if it's something you can learn how to get.

Why are so many people not happy? Well, there are lots of reasons. A person can be poor, sick, ugly, stupid… If we follow this logic then it would make sense to say that no one is happy since no one is perfect. But it must be that people can rise above their imperfections since there are happy people out there, I think that a person can be happy even when he is sad. This might sound like a contradiction to you. I guess it depends on your definition of happiness. How would you define happiness? Have you ever felt it?

happiness

It's been about two weeks since I last wrote and I've been thinking about what it means to be happy. I remember once seeing an old lady fall out of her wheelchair, and that was funny, actually hilarious. But I wasn't happy. The times I was drunk I can't remember. So I decided to go and investigate what happiness is.

The first person who I asked was a nineteen-year-old druggie in rehab. He told me that the happiest moment of his life was when he was fifteen. "You see," he said, "I was walkin' down the street and I saw me this women with a carriage tryin' to get up some stairs. I don't know why but I asked her if she needed a hand. She looked at me and smiled and said, 'I'd love one.' She invited me into her crib (house) and gave me a drink of water. She said that I was welcome in her house whenever I wanted. She was also the one who got me off the streets. I remember when I left her house I felt like I was 'trippin' on everything all at once, best feeling of my life."

The next person I asked was a "healthy looking" eighteen-year-old girl who I saw in the street. It took a few minutes for me to convince her that I wasn't playing a joke on her and really wanted to know what made her happy. She told me that last summer she was a counselor at a sleep-away camp for two months. She was in charge of a bunk with ten girls who were between the ages of thirteen and fifteen. She put all her effort in really trying to make an impact on their lives. Throughout the summer she didn't feel that she was getting any closer to the girls. By the time the last week came, she was ready to quit. On the last day of camp, when the busses were pulling up, she had a major shock. Every one of her girls was crying. They said that they would miss her so much. They promised to keep in touch. She said that she felt awesome. A week later she received letters from five different parents thanking her for giving their girls the best summer they ever had. She said that was the happiest week of her life.

I want to compare those two stories to one of my own. I was playing receiver in a football game. We were down by four points with nine seconds remaining in the game. We had to go thirty-two yards for a touchdown. In the huddle our quarterback looked at me and said, "It's coming to you." As I ran down the field I looked back and saw the ball coming. I realized that there was no way that I was going to catch it, it was way too far. At the last possible second I jumped; the ball hit my fingers and stayed in my hands! All of a sudden my friends were cheering and lifting me up on their shoulders. I had won the game for us.

Just thinking about that catch brings a smile to my face. Most people have a cool story where they got attention for a while. There is a big difference, though, between my story and the others. The catch I made wasn't something that I could do every day. If anything, it was a once-in-a-lifetime catch. I wasn't a better player or a better person after the game. I got lucky and it felt great.

Happiness has to be a constant feeling, not one you can tune into every now and then. When that guy walked away after helping that lady, he felt great about himself. He had lifted himself above his normal behavior and performed an act of kindness without any personal gain. It felt great! The world is full of nasty, uncaring people but there are still some decent ones out there, and for a minute he was one of them.

That girl at camp realized that her two months in camp weren't spent in vain. She realized that everything she did had an impact on those girls. She realized that she could be a role model for people.

If we try to put these feelings into words I think that the word would be "achievement." Everyone likes to feel achievement. The problem is that we focus on other things which we expect to bring us happiness, like wealth or fame. If we think for a minute we know the truth. There are so many billionaires who aren't happy, actors who are having affairs or killing themselves. In order to be happy you need to feel that you are achieving. You can feel achievement even when you're sad about something. How do you feel achievement? Achievement of what?

We can look at this from two angles. One is a physical aspect of achievement like climbing to the top of a mountain. The other is a spiritual achievement like prayer or acts of kindness. Both are very important and essential to the building up of a person.

When people feel that they are using their potential to their utmost capability they will be happier people. You don't have to get 100 on every test to be happy or feel worthwhile. If you work out and keep your body in shape, it's a great feeling; that's an achievement. (A fat man once told me that he was in shape, "Round is a shape, too.") By giving to others and helping others we are also achieving; we are making our world a better place. This is a job which every person should take upon himself, namely, to make his world a better place.

How many people do you interact with each day? Maybe twenty. If you can give each one of those people a smile or a nice word you can change their day, which in turn will affect many more people. Helping out in your surroundings is very effective. I don't know if you have ever noticed, but your mother is a much happier person when the house is clean. I'm a different person if music is playing when I walk into my apartment. This is our job: to make our own little world into a better place for ourselves and for others.

Dennis Prager, a talk-show host, once gave the following analogy to show how warped values are:

If a parent has to choose between two high schools, one is noted for their stellar academic achievement (your kid has a good shot at going to Harvard) and the other boasts a top-notch athletic department (maybe the kid will earn a football scholarship to Michigan), where would he send his son? Most would send to the academic school.

What if there were a third school whose athletic and academic areas were weak, but which churned out young men and women of outstanding character. Would he send his son there? Most wouldn't, even though society pays lip service to the idea of ethics and morals having primacy.

There is also the spiritual aspect of working on ourselves, whether through prayer or religion. People try to find meaning for their very existence. Setting small goals to work on your self-improvement is essential to your growth. No one can just jump into something without taking small steps first. You can try if you want to, but its stupid.

It's sort of like climbing a mountain. You are taught that you look for a hole and stick your pick into it. One approach is to make sure your pick is sturdy before you put weight on it and then look for another hole. Sometimes you will find a hole a little to the side or lower down. This doesn't mean you are moving backwards, because it is all part of your climb to the top.

The other approach is you see a hole twenty feet up. You jump and put your pick in the hole, but it's not sturdy and you fall and break your neck. You are never going to climb again.

By taking things slowly we balance ourselves and our progress to make sure that we don't take on too much. The feeling of achievement is always there because you know you are growing and moving in a positive direction.

So you ask me if you can be happy? The answer is "definitely." It will take some work and it's not necessarily easy, but if you want it you can have it. It's up to you to be happy. Make your life and world a happier place; this is what life is all about.

part three

straighttalk

straightalk

I n this third and final part of my book, I'm going to share with you some ideas which I have collected from various people whom I greatly respect. Over the last couple of months I have worked very hard to instill these ideas into my life. They have affected me to a certain extent. I hope they will do the same for you.

To be honest, I've written this book more for myself than for anyone else. I wanted to sort out my own ideas about growing up, to help me get to know myself better. At this point I don't know if this book will be a hit or not; after all, I'm just a teenager.

I've debated with myself whether to write my name as the author of this book. On the one hand, I've tried to be honest and straightforward with you until now and want to continue doing so. On the other hand, I'm not a doctor or psychologist who probably knows what he is talking about. I decided that I wouldn't use my name. Instead I have opened an e-mail account for anyone who would like to be in contact with me: straightalkft2t@hotmail.com.

This third part is my favorite part, and most important to me. It means that I've actually finished something. I have never finished anything before. I've never finished school or seen anything through before, so this really means a lot to me.

I have to thank my parents, family, and close friends for pushing me along the way to continue writing. Without you guys I never would have been able to do this. I also want to thank YOU for listening to me. I hope I wasn't a bore. I'd really love to hear from you and your feedback on my book.

In the first part of the book I tried to talk about how we think others view us. In the second part I spoke about how we view ourselves. I'm not beating around the bush with my questions, rather I've tried to talk straight and be honest with you. I hope that your conclusion is the same as mine, namely, that there are things you can change, and you can be a happy person with a slightly different outlook.

It has been a lot of fun and a big challenge writing this book. I hope you enjoy and find this last part as helpful as I did.

appreciating what
we have

f we were to take a survey and ask people "What are the important things in life?" most people would probably answer
"Money, brains, and good looks."

   If we look a little deeper it would appear that this answer is
way off. What is really important is that we can breathe, hear, see, talk,
love, cry, etc. The problem is that we forget about the real obvious
everyday things and take them for granted. Let me ask you, if you met
a person who had all the money in the world but was blind, would you
trade your eyes for all that money?

The master was sitting with his disciples in the lobby of a hotel. He was in the midst of explaining the wonders of life, when he suddenly paused in mid-sentence. "Look," he said. He pointed to a vase on one of the tables."Aren't they beautiful?" There were flowers in the vase, and they were truly colorful, lively, beautiful flowers. Silence pervaded for another minute, as everyone was contemplating the previously unnoticed charm of nature's color.

The silence was broken by the master's insight. "This," he said, "is really the point I'm trying to teach. The flowers were here all along. Their brilliant colors were available to see, yet we were too busy with other matters; we were blind to their grace. Only when I pointed them out, when our focus was shifted to what was in front of our eyes, only then was their beauty actualized, the mission of their color accomplished.

"It was always there, yet not utilized. My teachings," he continued, "do not come to establish new principles, I'm not inventing previously unknown concepts. All I am striving for is to point out what it is that we already have. Focus on it. Utilize its potential. Don't let it go unnoticed. In a nutshell, that is my life's message."

focus on the good

The first and most important guideline for attaining happiness is learning to focus on the good. Everyone's life includes positive and negative aspects. As a matter of fact, as you are reading these words, you can make a short mental list for yourself, the good things on one side, the not-so-good things on the other.

So how can I be happy? What about all my problems? If you're trying to convince me that everything is great, that I've got no troubles…you're nuts!

Let me explain.

You can have two people in the exact same situation. Same joys, same pains. Same opportunities and same troubles. So, what is the real difference? Their approach. Their focus.

If you ask one guy: "What's doing? What is really going on in your life?" He will reply by telling you all his troubles. He isn't lying, he really has these problems. Yet another fellow in the same situation will give a totally different answer. What he will say is that everything is great, life is good even though he doesn't deserve it. Is he lying? Does he not have problems?

It really all boils down to this: we all know that the optimist sees the cup half full while the pessimist sees it half empty. So, who is right, objectively speaking? Seemingly they are both right. The cup really is half empty and half full. So what is the difference?

My observation is as follows: the optimist truly has his cup filled to overflowing. The pessimist sees a half-empty cup, but truly his cup is completely empty. And we are still talking about the same cup!

That's powerful. The optimist is living in the positive. His focus is always on the positive, the good, the uplifting. And where a person's focus is — that is what his life experiences consist of.

So, neither one is lying. Yet the description each one gives is so radically different, and yet they are both right.

You've got problems? So does everyone else. Readjust your lens, look only at the good, and live in it. Your cup is overflowing with goodness. If you choose to filter your problems out of your perception, your positive attitude is the filter that will let the goodness pour, without the impurities.

That doesn't mean you should ignore your problems, that's foolish. Of course you have to be practical, you have to do what needs to be done. But dealing with problems should be just rational, not emotional. Don't get caught up with it. Allow your emotional focus to rest only on what lifts your spirit, not what makes it sag.

don't speak about your problems

This might not apply to everyone, but I feel that it's important to include. A lot of times when people do something wrong they feel that they have to tell everyone about what they did. You might think that this is because they feel bad about what they did, which may be true, but that is not the reason that they talk. What they are really doing is making the issue bigger than it really is. In a sense they are showing off. By telling people about what they did, they convince themselves that they are bad and what they did was bad.

A friend of mine told me recently that when he was doing some work for the FBI, he was shocked when he walked into the main building. He had expected to see a lot of machines and fancy equipment. Instead all he saw was a coffee machine and some computers. He asked one of the people working there where all the technology and equipment was, like on TV and the movies. "After all," he said, "isn't that how you catch the bad guys?"

The worker answered, "The way we catch people is, people talk, someone always talks."

When we do something wrong we want to tell others about what we did. (That is why the first rule about breaking rules is to do it by yourself. Do it with a crowd and people will find out.)

If you do something which really bothers you, instead of talking about it with all your friends, try not to talk about it. Most of the time you will see that you are making a bigger issue out of it than it really is. (You can talk to your mentor about it or even a close friend. Just don't go blab to every person you know.)

know who you're not

When we were little we all had dreams of who and what we wanted to be when we grew up. Boys wanted to be policemen, superman, or an astronaut. Girls wanted to be ballerinas, nurses, or models. (Personally, I wanted to be a fire truck.)

Very few of us are lucky enough to have those dreams come true. Most of us, even by the time we go to college, still have no clue as to what we want to do in life.

Every single person knows what he or she doesn't want to do. If you get sick every time you see blood then you shouldn't be a doctor. If you are scared of heights you definitely won't be a pilot. Sometimes, by discarding unappealing activities, we can hone in on more appealing ones.

The same is true when trying to get to know yourself. By finding out who you're not, it will make it easier for you to find out who you are.

People are always moving and changing professions. This doesn't change who they are. A person always has the ability to work on himself or herself to become a better person. However this is only possible if you have a direction, which you have chosen for yourself.

To give an example: when trying to decide which profession is suitable for you, first you must knock out what you don't want, and you'll probably be left with two or three options. Most people will then ask themselves, "Well, where will I be the happiest?" This is a really dumb question. The place you are in won't make you happy if you don't emanate happiness. You have to be a happy person, and be content with yourself.

If you are stuck and can't decide what to do with yourself, my suggestion is one that is very important for every single person. And that is…

having a mentor

To have a mentor means a person whom you trust, look up to, and can relate to. It's a struggle to find such a person. A lot of times we don't find the right person on our first try. A mentor isn't your best friend and isn't meant to be. He is someone whom you try to emulate. He is also someone who, when he tells you to do something, you do it. It is, therefore, smart not to have more than one person like this. You can have lots of people who you respect, to talk to and learn from, but only one teacher.

What you want out of a mentor is someone who knows you better than you know yourself, whose concern is for you to succeed in life by becoming a good person. His job isn't to make your decisions for you, only to clear away the cobwebs and wrong reasoning which blind you from making a good decision. A mentor (like a parent) might not always approve of what you are doing, but will always be there behind you.

The reason a mentor is so important is because he is a person you can share all your feelings with, without having to worry about getting in trouble or disapproval. He also has more knowledge and life experience than you and can therefore open up your eyes to things which you were unable to see before. The ideal mentor is a father or mother. A lot of us can't feel the same feeling of openness with our parents as we can with someone else. That is fine. Go and find that person. It might not be easy, but I promise you that it's worth it.

make your issues
someone else's

When faced with a problem, most realistic people will tell you that you can't run from it. "The only way to solve a problem is by tackling it head-on."

This is true, but when you believe that you have lots of problems, it can be very hard to look them all in the face. When we are faced with lots of problems we get scared and depressed. We know that running away from them won't solve them, and eventually they will catch up with us much more severely than before. Yet when we are faced with them, we don't see any way of solving them.

Let me suggest something which might sound a little funny. I don't know if it's a guaranteed success, but I know a few people who tried it and liked the idea.

Take out a piece of paper, and write down everything that is bothering you. It can be things which you don't like about yourself and want to change, or it can be problems that you are having in school or at home. After you have written down everything that is on your mind, put the piece of paper in an envelope and seal it. Then put it in your closet or drawer.

After a week has passed, take out that envelope. Look at it as if you just received a letter from a close friend whom you really like a lot. In this letter your friend is telling you all about their problems, and is asking you for help in solving them. (You can probably relate to your friend's problems because they are a lot like your own.) Write down on another piece of paper your suggestions and answers to your friend's letter.

We all know from experience that it's easier to find an answer for someone else than it is for ourselves. Sometimes, by removing ourselves from our problems, we can have an easier time finding solutions.

having a secret

One terrific way of building self-esteem is by feeling special. If you had something that no one else had, you would probably feel very special. I would like to give you something that only you can have and no one else can touch. It's called a secret. You see, some people keep all their feelings inside themselves, which isn't always so good. Sometimes we need someone to talk to or even just a hug from a friend. By keeping all your emotions inside, you could be hurting yourself. On the other hand, you have people who go and tell everybody about what is going on in their lives. This is a very bad thing to do because you have nothing that is yours; your life is on display for everyone. You lose your individuality.

If you are this type of person, you probably don't keep secrets very well. By keeping a secret of a friend you are showing trust. By having a secret which belongs to you, you are making yourself into an individual. What I mean by a secret is doing something that no one else knows about, whether it's helping at home without telling anyone what you did, or volunteering at an old age home without anyone knowing about it.

You might ask me, "What is wrong with telling people what I do?"

My answer is very simple. By telling people the things that you do, in a sense you are showing off. "Look how great I am! I do this." Not telling anyone about your actions makes what you are doing so much more special. You are doing something that involves no selfishness.

Take one thing, something small and easy, but something that you can do and stick with. Don't tell anyone ever. This is your secret. Keep it and appreciate it.

the ten things

I was wondering how to end the book. I guess I got very lucky because my cousin called me up today complaining about her life. She said that she was always unhappy. She felt that her friends didn't really appreciate her. She also seemed to be very confused as to which direction she was taking in life.

I'm not going to go into all the details of her very interesting life. My first reaction was to tell her to read this book. It seemed that almost everything that was bothering her was discussed in here. The reason I didn't tell her to read this was because she was looking for answers. This book doesn't supply answers; it was written to help you find your own answers.

So instead I asked her what she was doing right now. She said,

"Nothing." I told her that that wasn't true. "Right now you are breathing, talking, seeing…these are all amazing things which not everyone is lucky enough to be able to do."

I don't know if she got what I was trying to tell her. Make a list of ten things that you have which you can be thankful for. It can be your nose or waterbed or anything else you can think of. Over the next ten days take one of those things and imagine what life would be like without it.

We all have so much to be thankful for. Life is meant to be enjoyed. Let's live it, every second of it. Get a move on; find some meaning in your life. You can do it, you have what it takes to succeed and be happy.

What are you waiting for?